Mel Bay's

Bass Scales in Tablature

By Jim Betts

1 2 3 4 5 6 7 8 9 0

FOREWORD

This book was written to serve three purposes:

- To provide bassists with an "escape" from being anchored to one position on the bass neck, and improve left-hand technique;

- To familiarize bass players with notes and patterns throughout the entire range of the instrument;

- To help in understanding and hearing modes and scales in all twelve keys.

Each scale group is presented in a "circle of fifths" format, starting with the scale or mode with no accidentals, in notation and tablature. The numbers in italics below the tablature are suggested fingerings, chosen for smoothness, use of all fingers, and increased mastery of position shifting on the neck.

Since there are several popular configurations of strings and frets for the electric bass, I arbitrarily chose to arrange these scales and modes for a four-string bass with a 21-fret neck (the "Fender bass" setup). If you have 22 or 24 frets, or if you use a five- or six-string instrument, these patterns will still serve to increase fingerboard mobility, and you may find ways to extend the given patterns to fit your particular instrument.

Jim Betts
September 16, 1995

CONTENTS

Major Scales

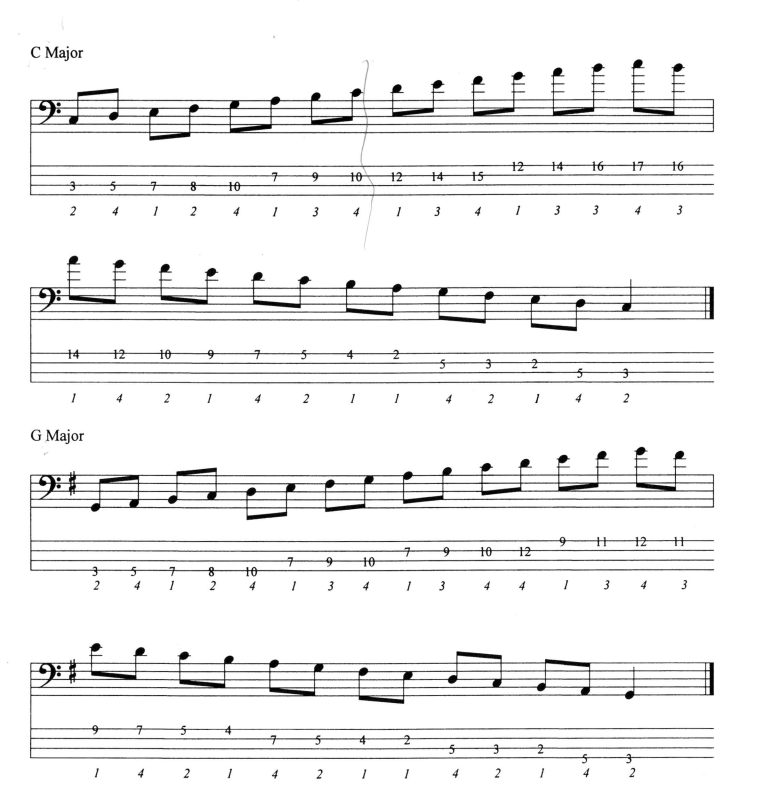

D Major

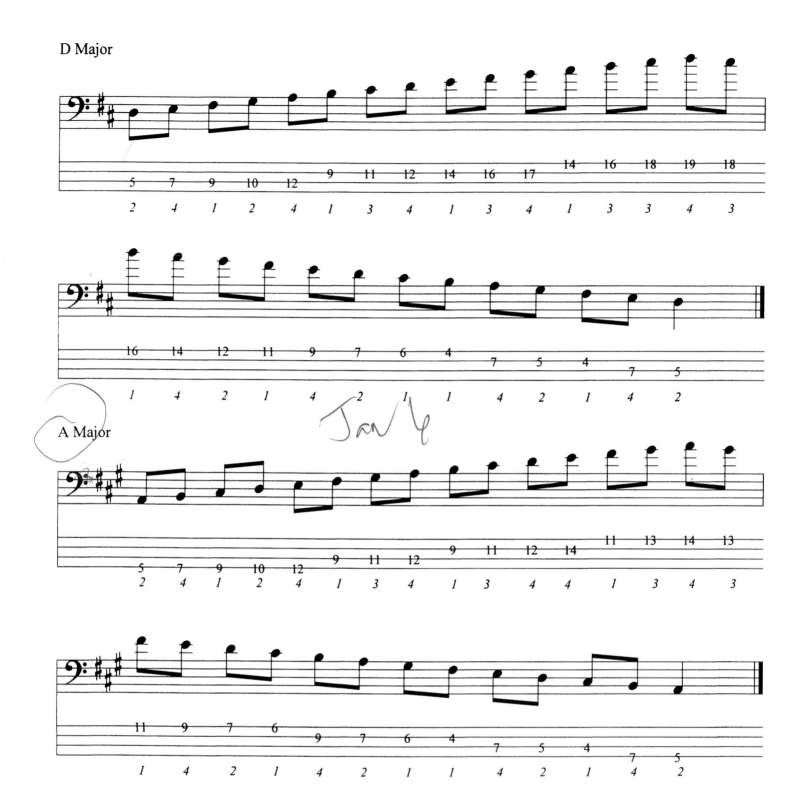

A Major

4

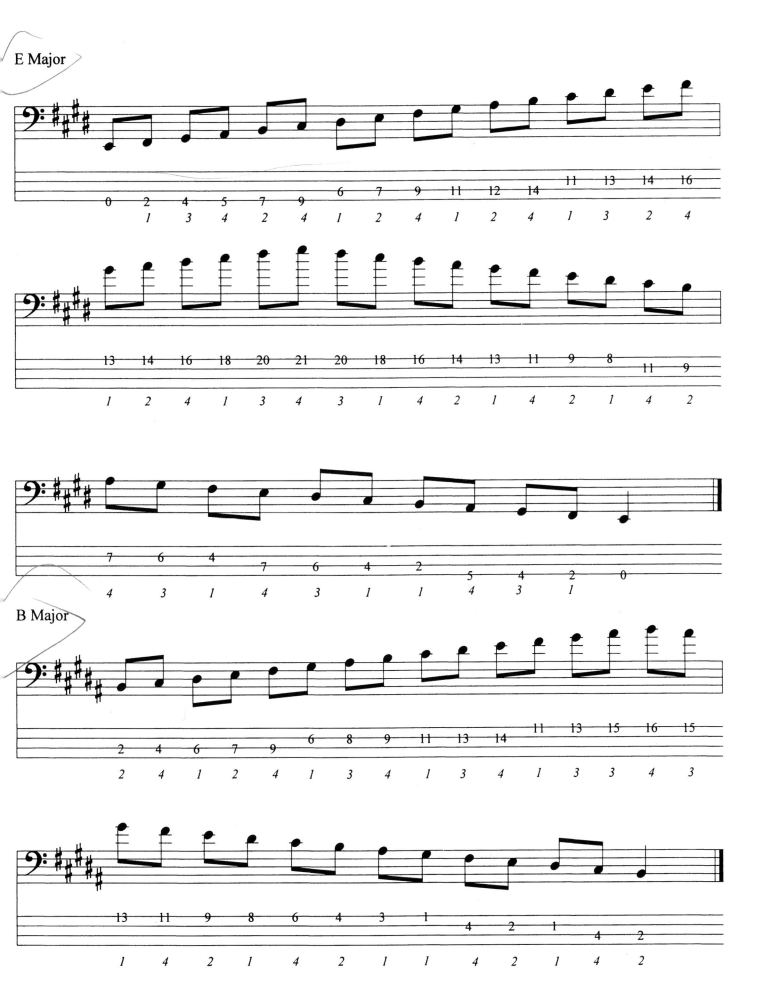

F-Sharp Major

D-Flat Major

6

A-Flat Major

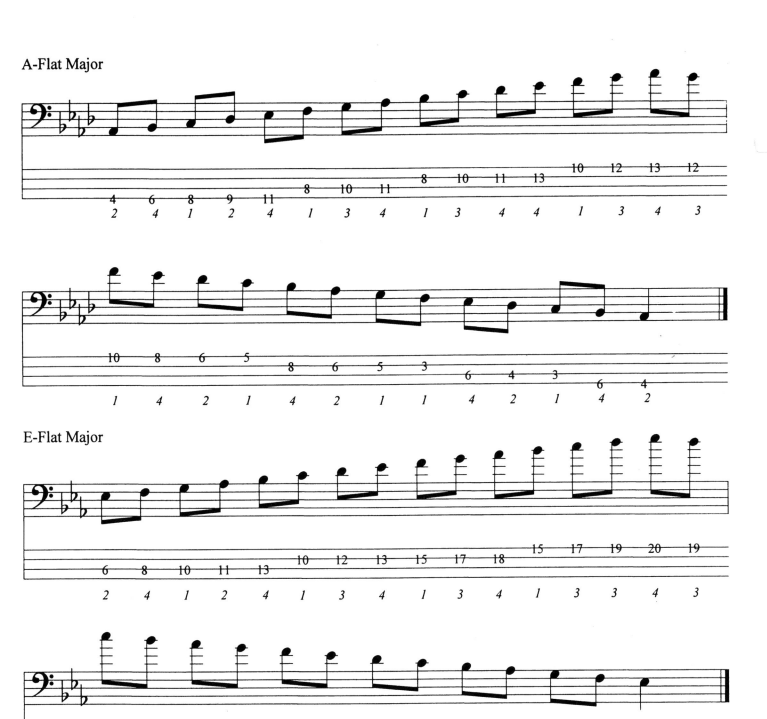

E-Flat Major

B-Flat Major

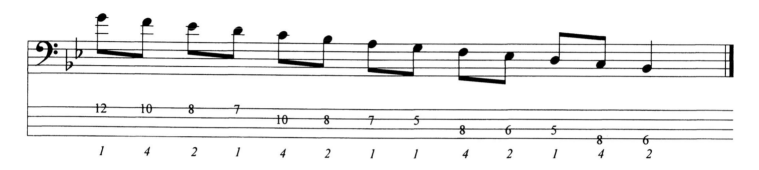

F Major

Dorian Modes

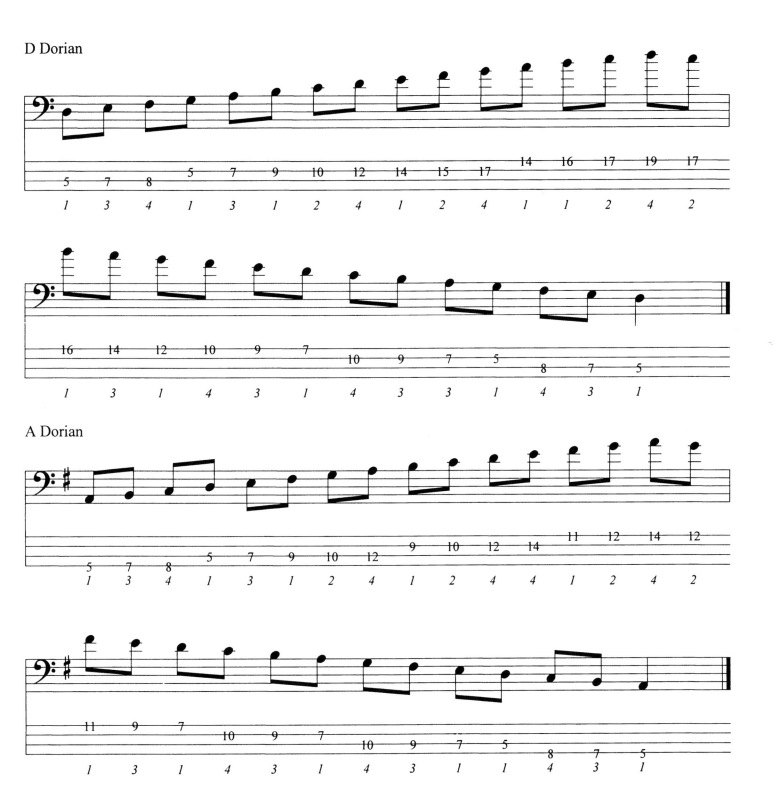

9

E Dorian

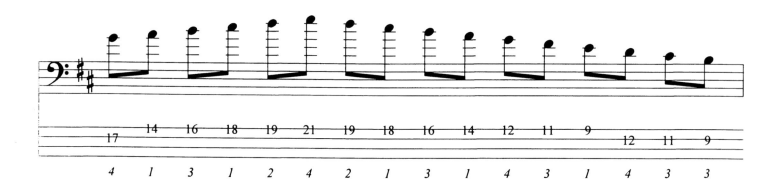

B Dorian

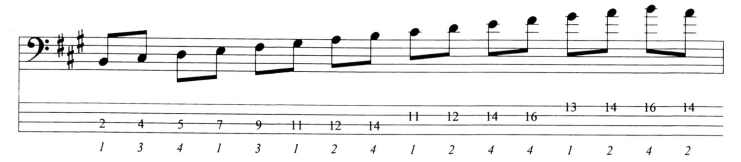

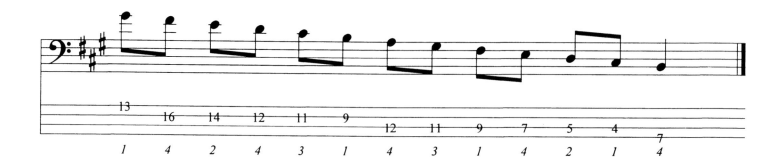

F-Sharp Dorian

C-Sharp Dorian

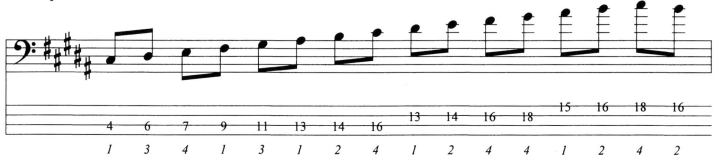

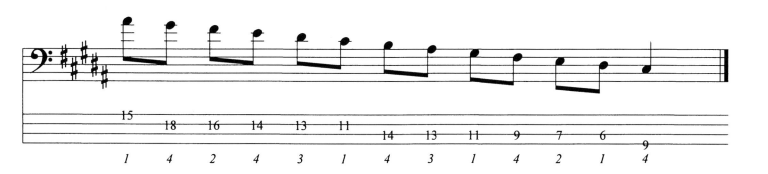

G-Sharp Dorian

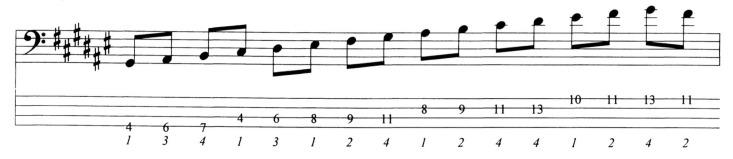

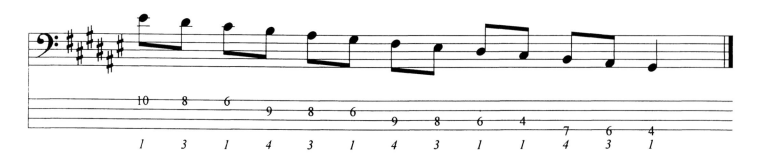

E-Flat Dorian

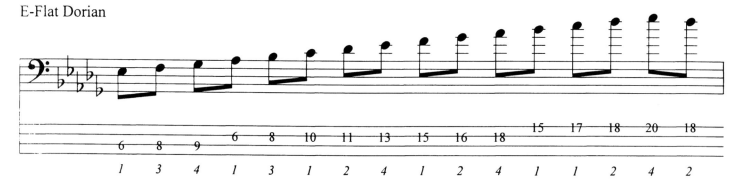

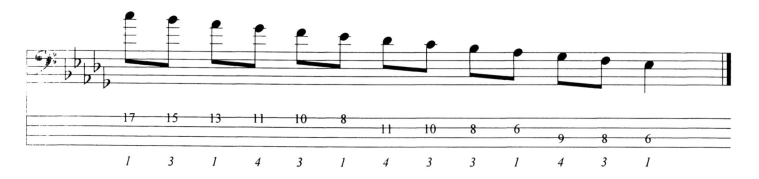

B-Flat Dorian

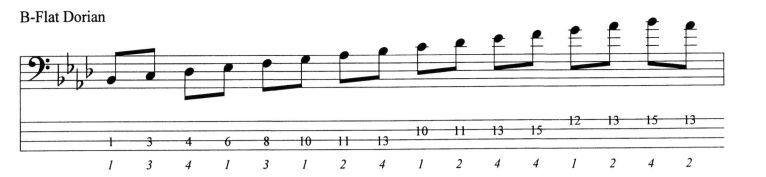

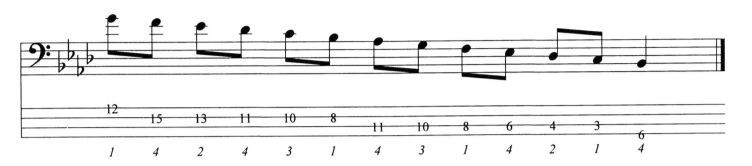

F Dorian

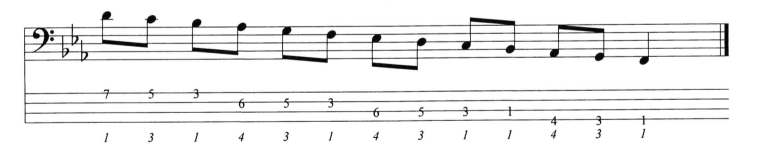

C Dorian

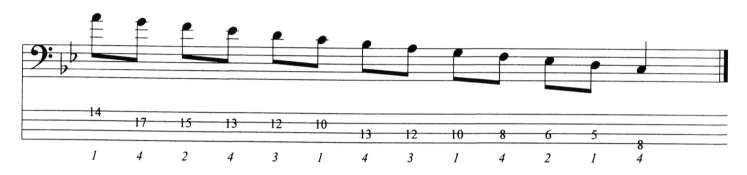

G Dorian

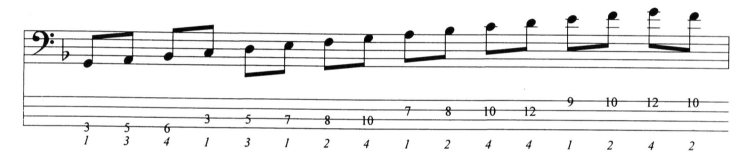

14

Phrygian Modes

E Phrygian

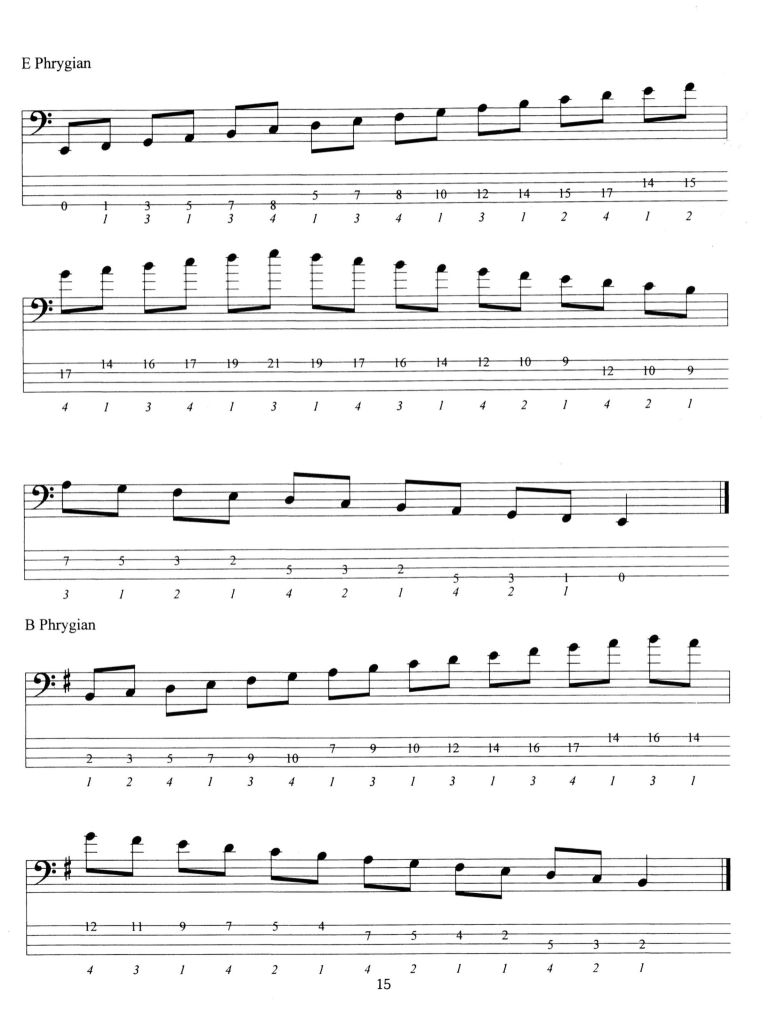

B Phrygian

F-Sharp Phrygian

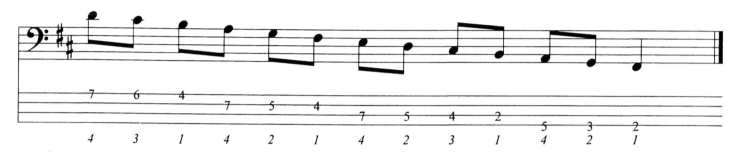

C-Sharp Phrygian

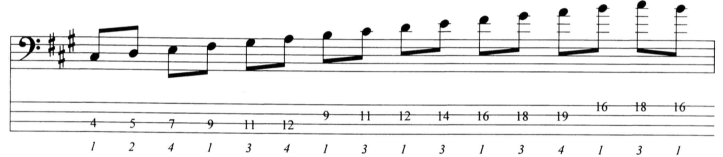

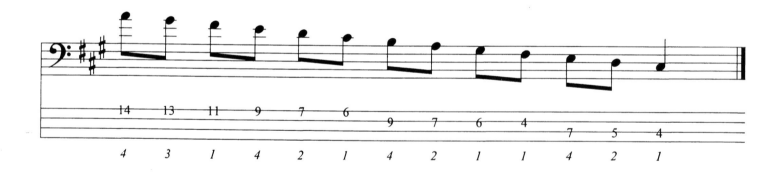

G-Sharp Phrygian

D-Sharp Phrygian

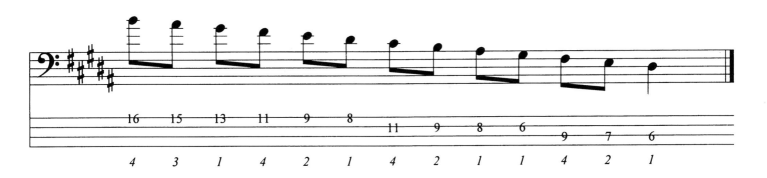

17

B-Flat Phrygian

F Phrygian

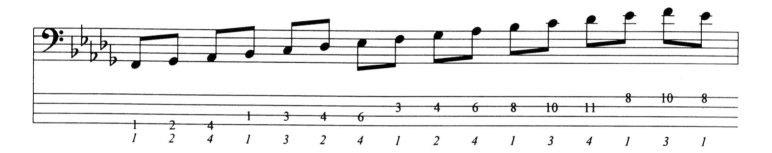

C Phrygian

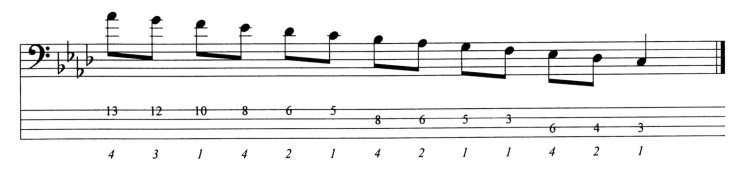

G Phrygian

D Phrygian

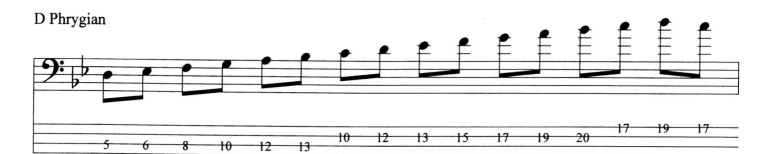

A Phrygian

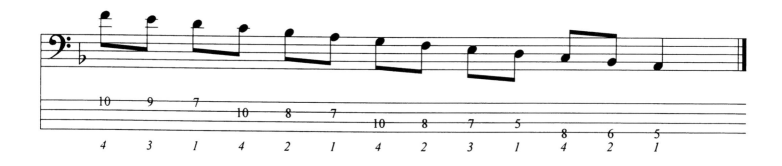

20

Lydian Modes

F Lydian

C Lydian

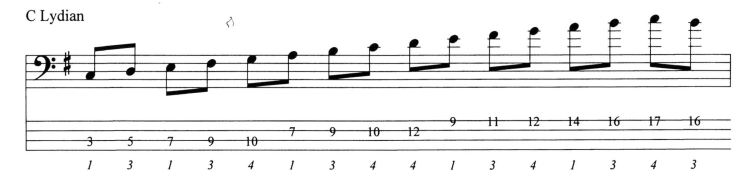

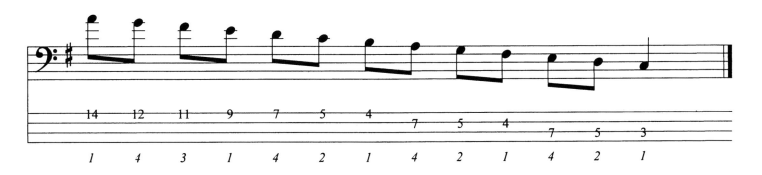

G Lydian

D Lydian

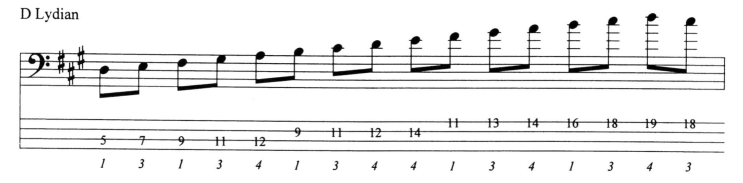

A Lydian

E Lydian

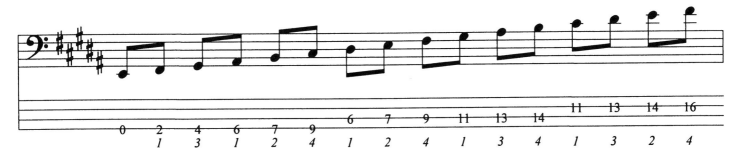

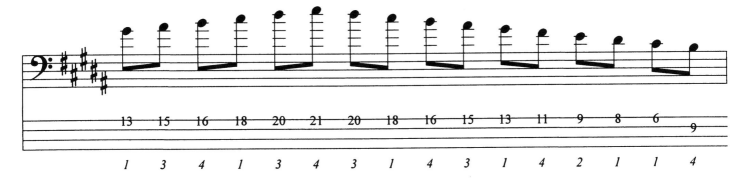

23

B Lydian

G-Flat Lydian

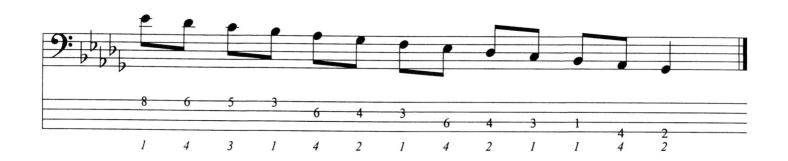

24

D-Flat Lydian

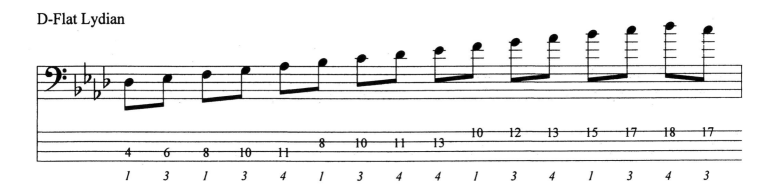

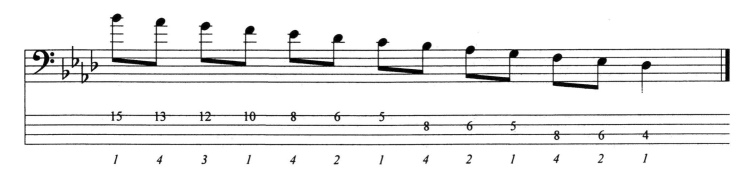

A-Flat Lydian

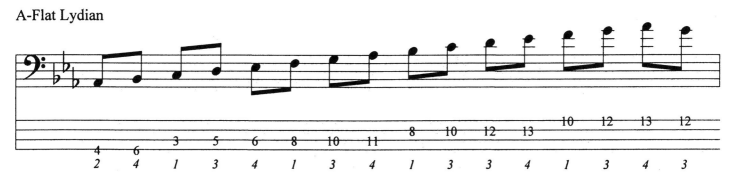

E-Flat Lydian

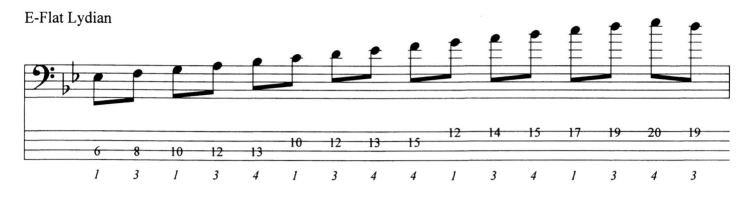

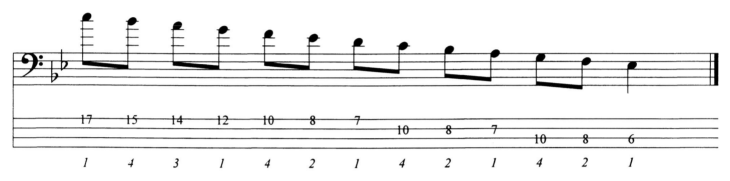

B-Flat Lydian

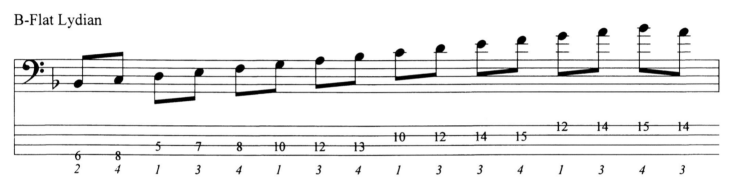

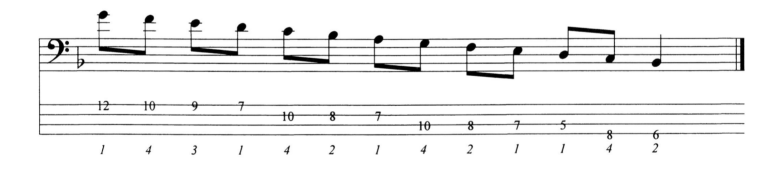

Mixolydian Modes

G Mixolydian

D Mixolydian

27

A Mixolydian

E Mixolydian

B Mixolydian

F-Sharp Mixolydian

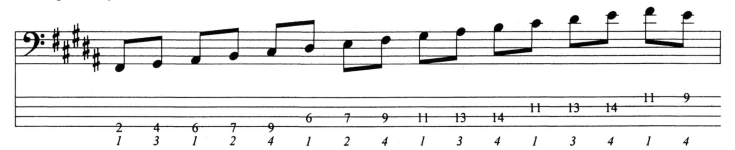

D-Flat Mixolydian

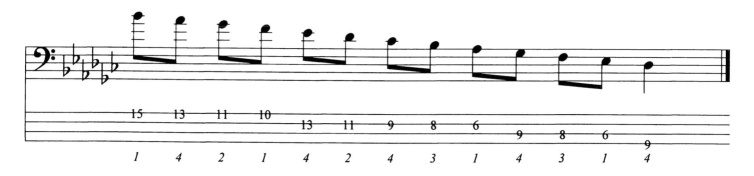

A-Flat Mixolydian

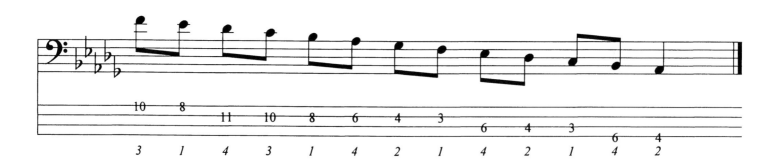

E-Flat Mixolydian

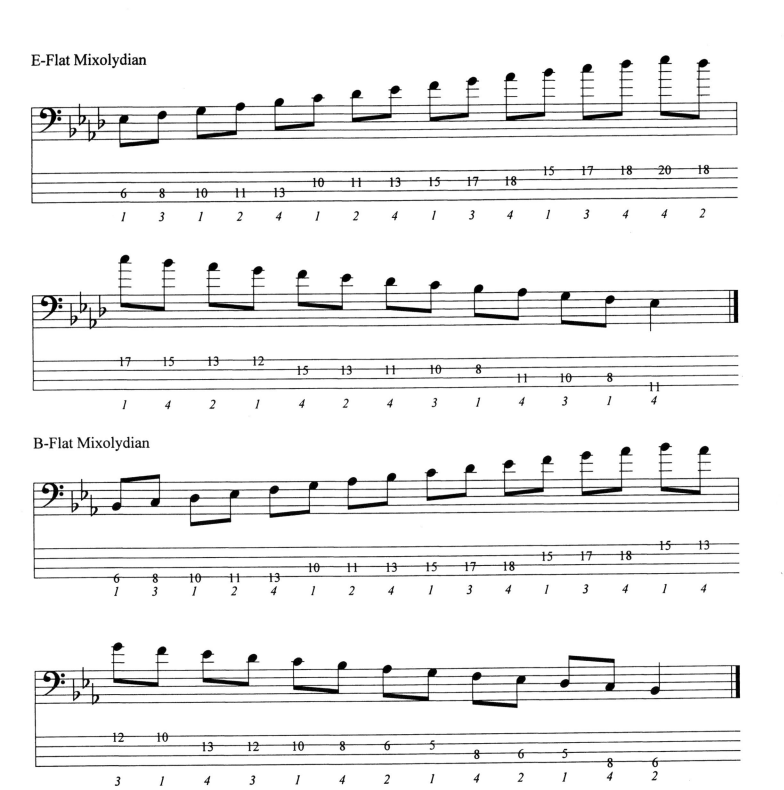

B-Flat Mixolydian

F Mixolydian

C Mixolydian

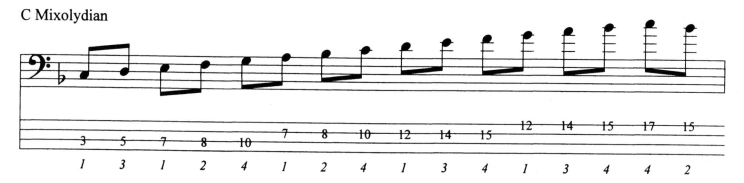

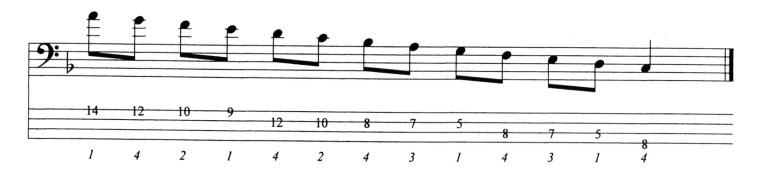

32

Natural Minor (Aeolian Mode) Scales

A Minor

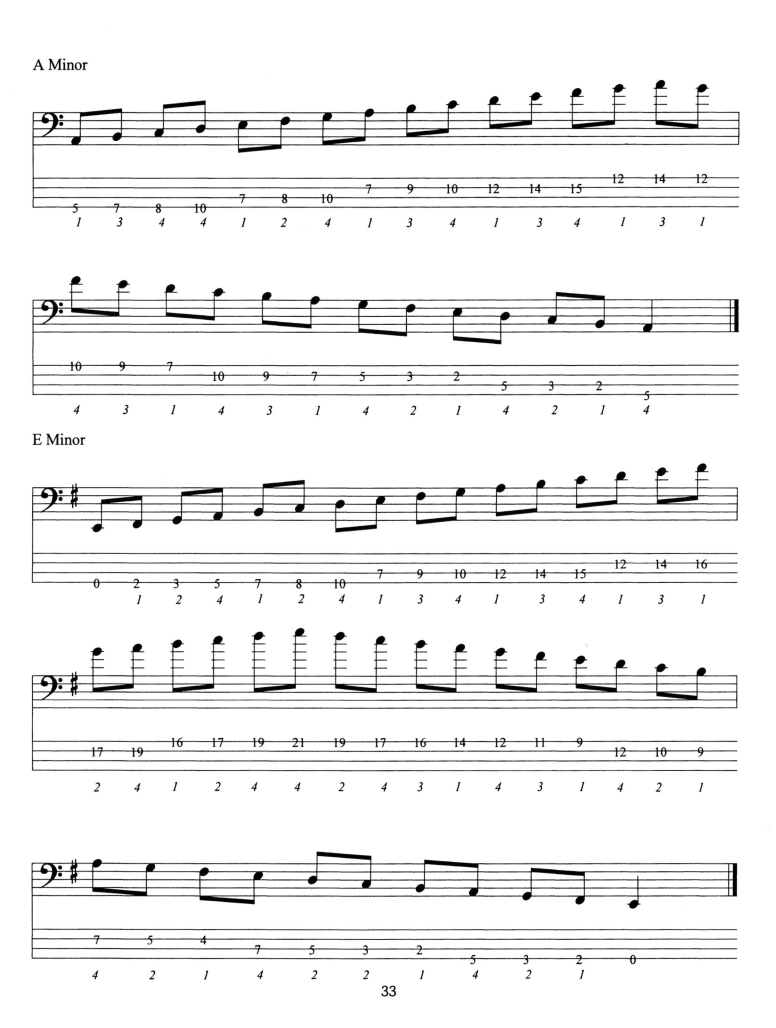

E Minor

B Minor

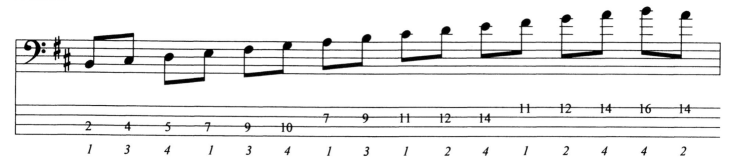

F-Sharp Minor

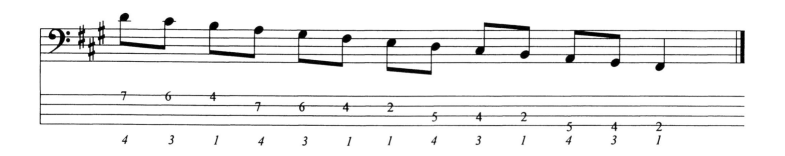

C-Sharp Minor

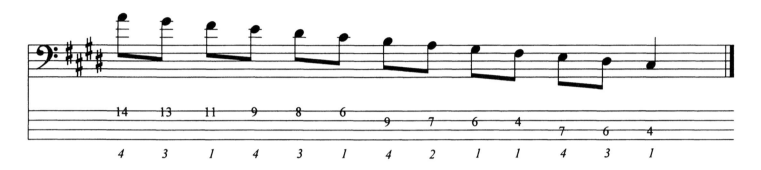

G-Sharp Minor

E-Flat Minor

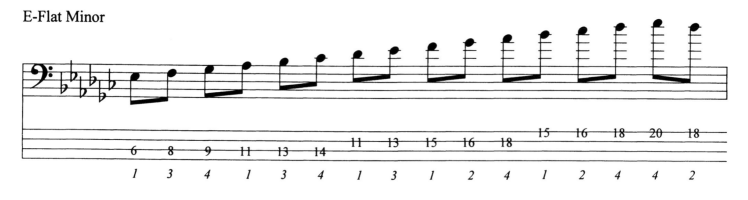

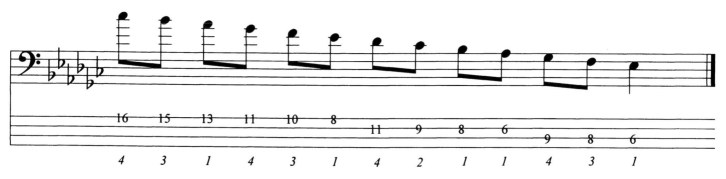

B-Flat Minor

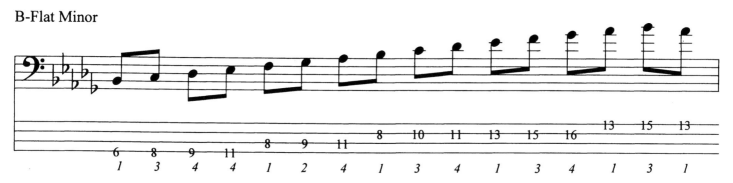

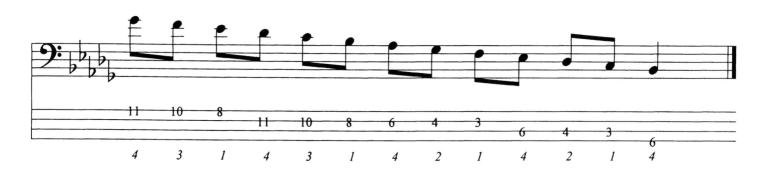

F Minor

C Minor

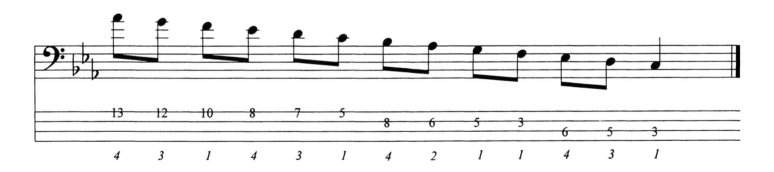

G Minor

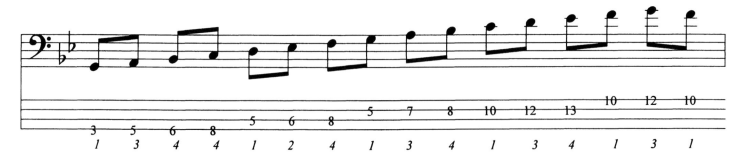

D Minor

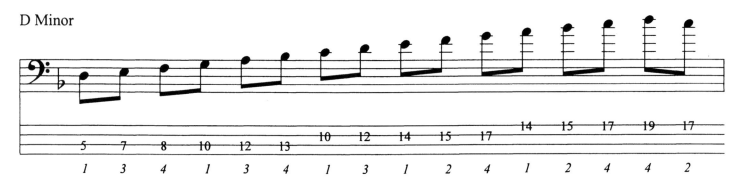

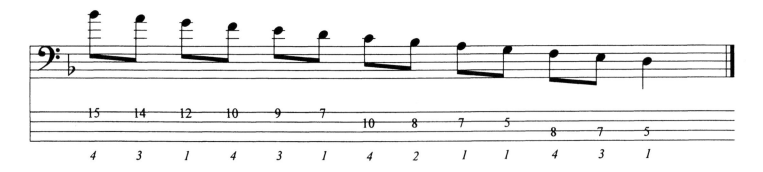

Melodic Minor Scales

A Melodic Minor

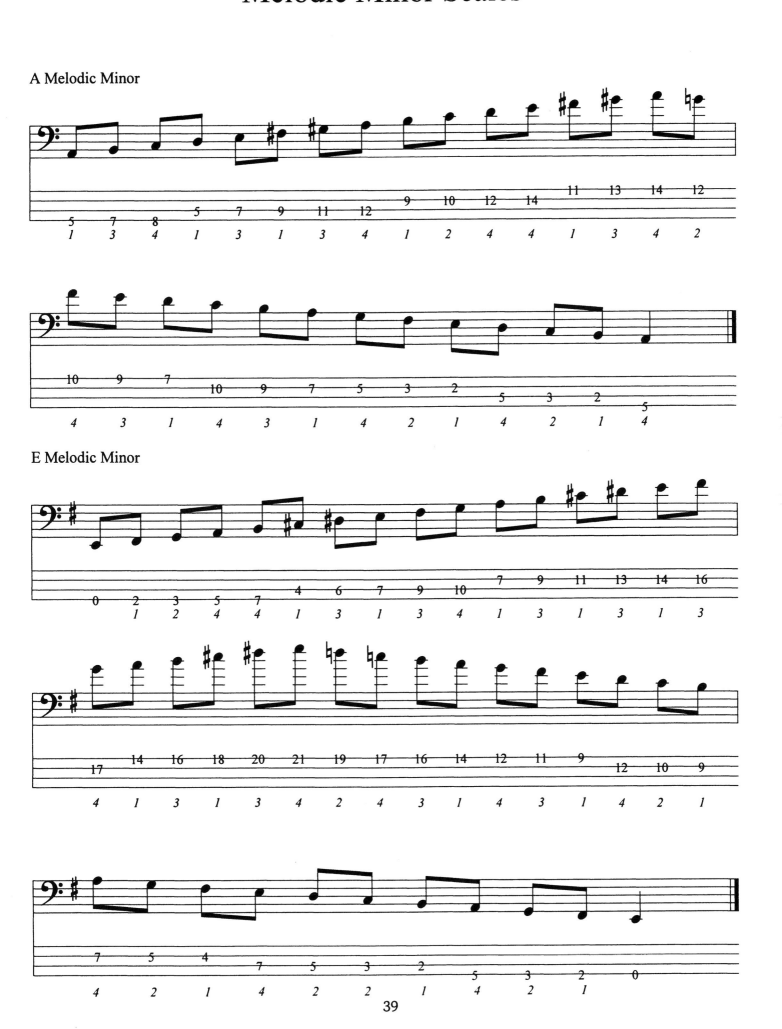

E Melodic Minor

39

B Melodic Minor

F-Sharp Melodic Minor

40

C-Sharp Melodic Minor

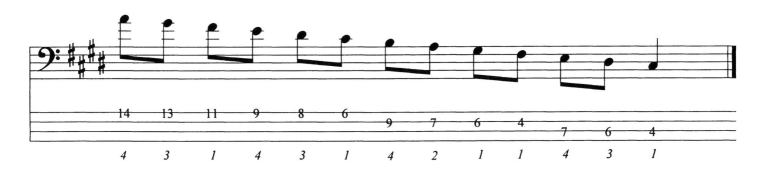

G-Sharp Melodic Minor

E-Flat Melodic Minor

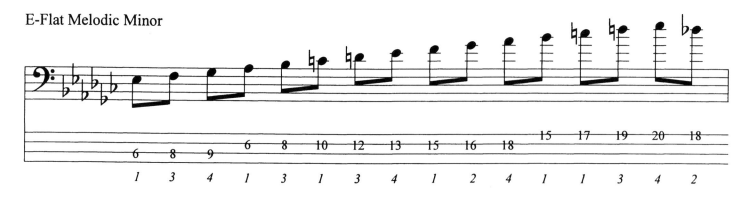

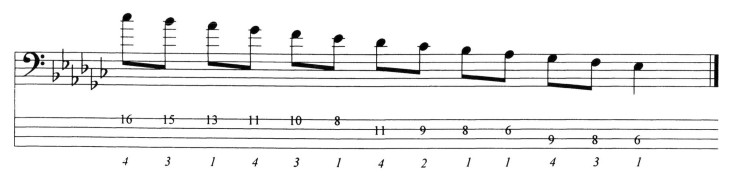

B-Flat Melodic Minor

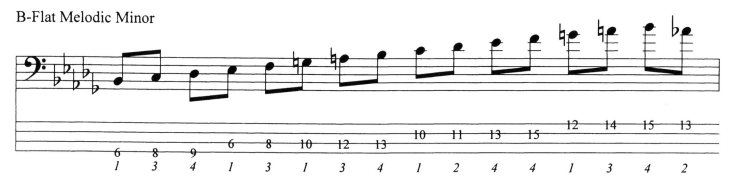

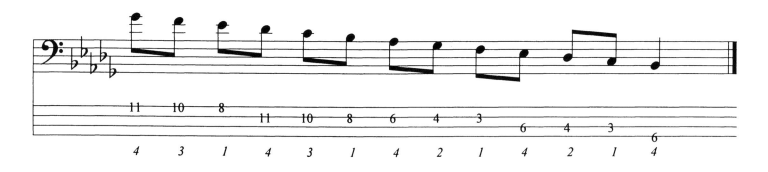

F Melodic Minor

C Melodic Minor

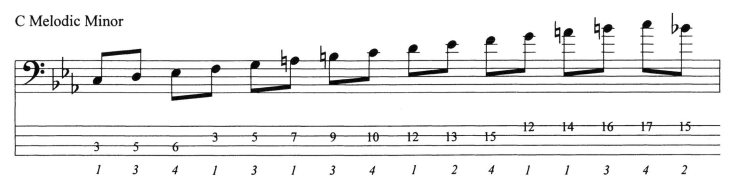

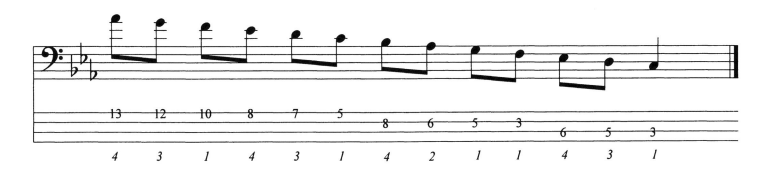

43

G Melodic Minor

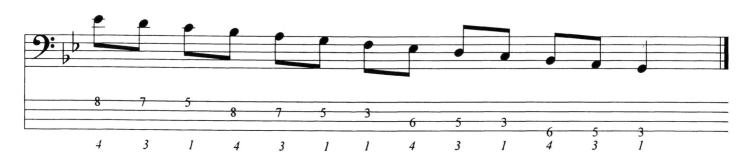

D Melodic Minor

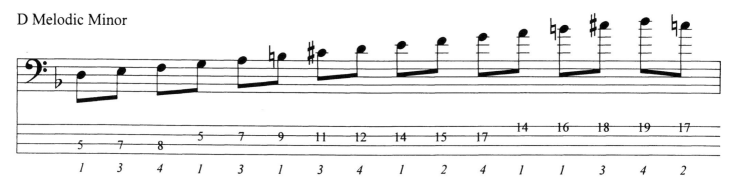

44

Major Pentatonic Scales

C Major

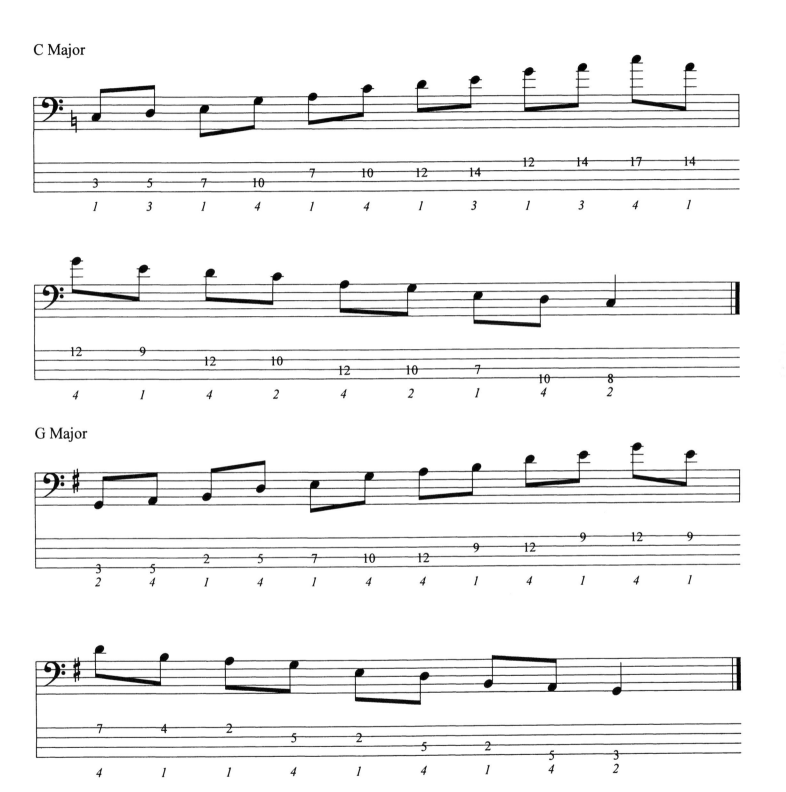

G Major

D Major

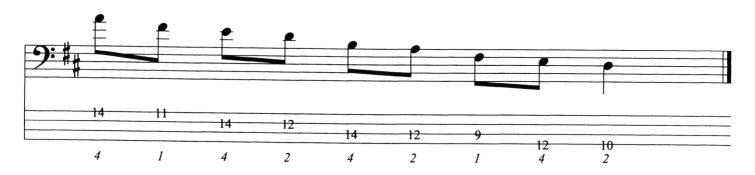

A Major

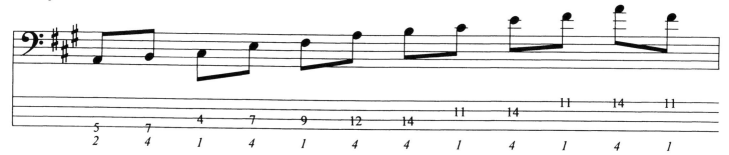

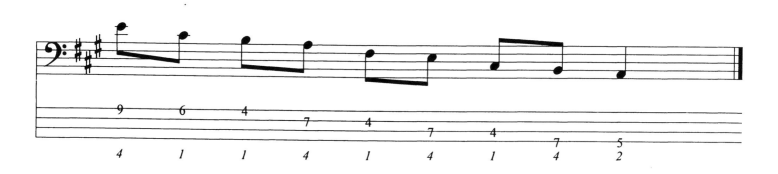

E Major

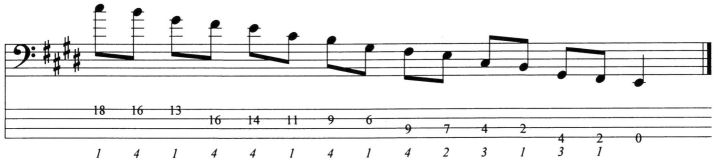

B Major

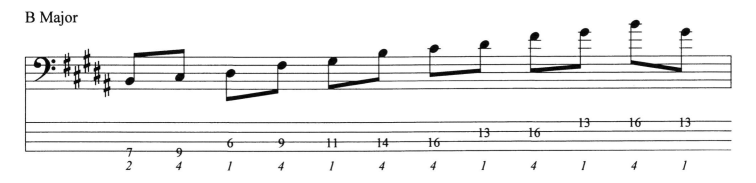

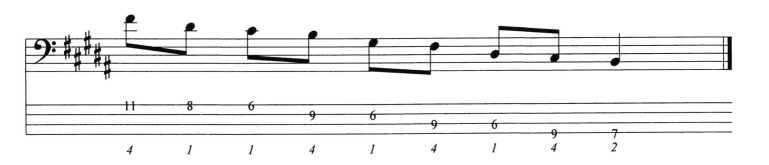

F-Sharp Major

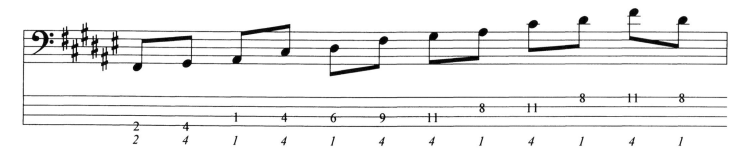

D-Flat Major

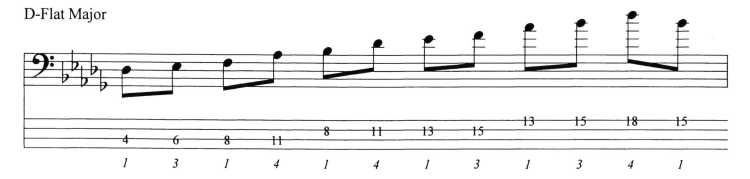

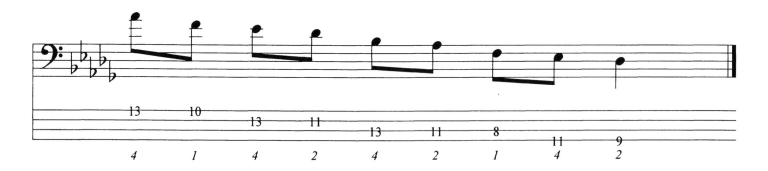

A-Flat Major

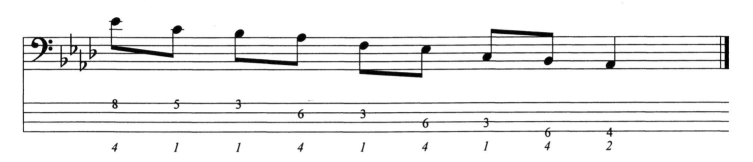

E-Flat Major

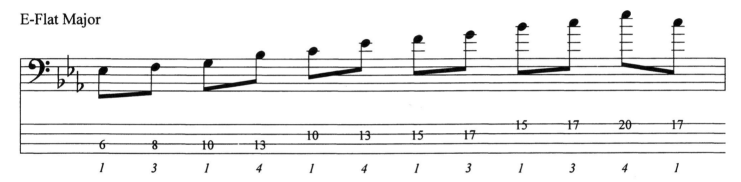

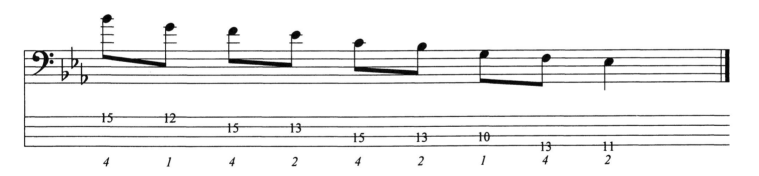

B-Flat Major

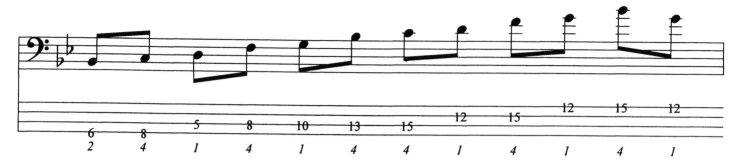

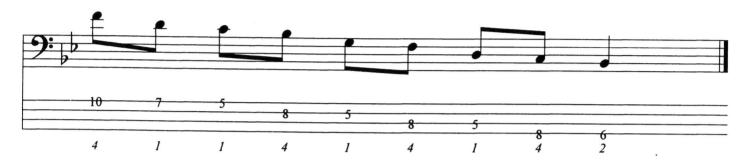

F Major

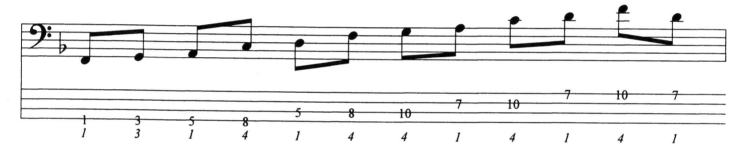

Minor Pentatonic Scales

A Minor

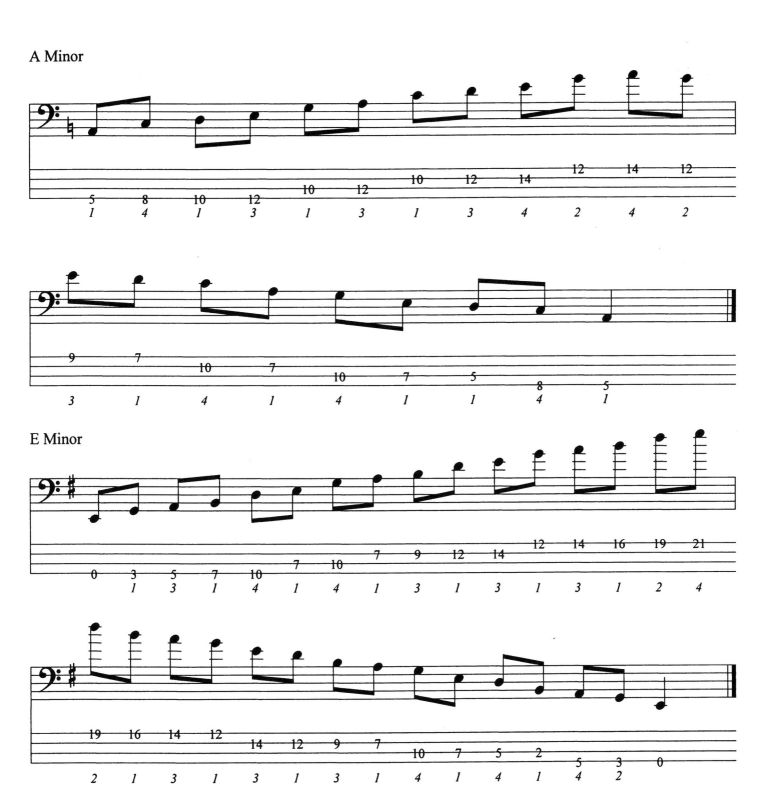

E Minor

B Minor

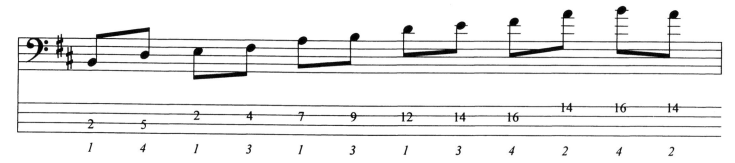

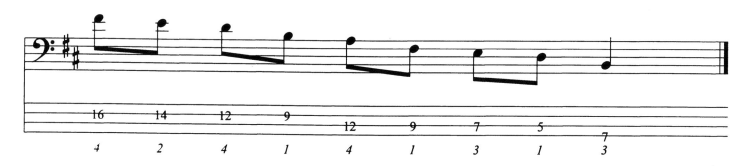

F-Sharp Minor

C-Sharp Minor

G-Sharp Minor

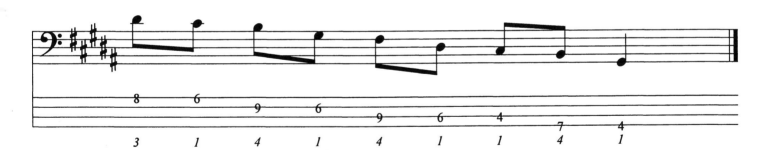

E-Flat Minor

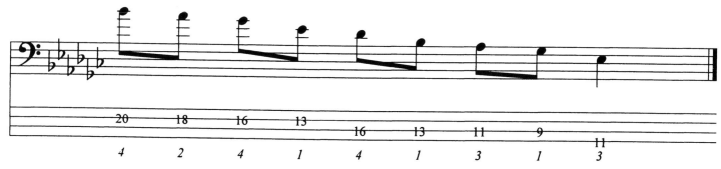

B-Flat Minor

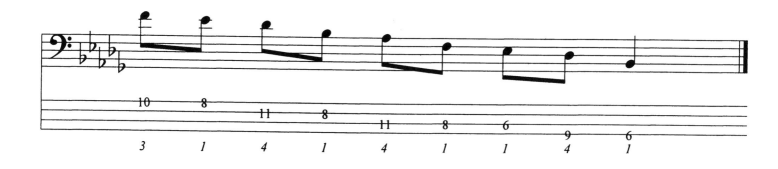

54

F Minor

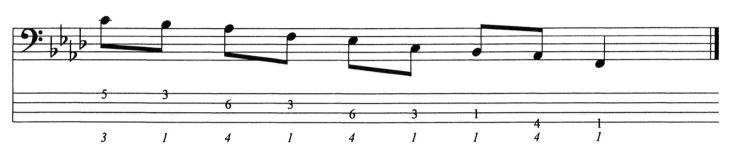

C Minor

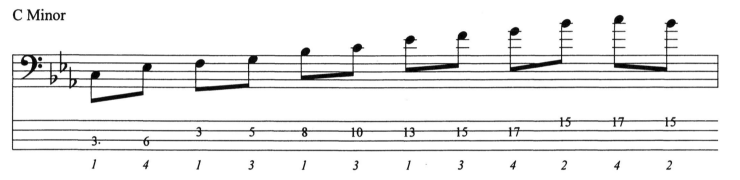

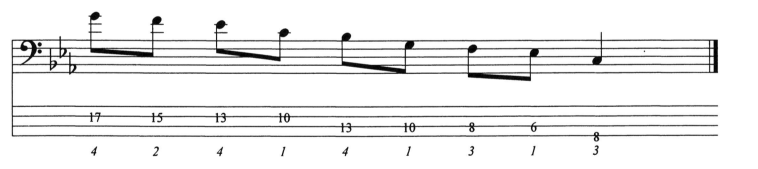

G Minor

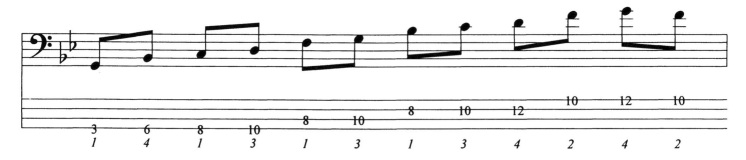

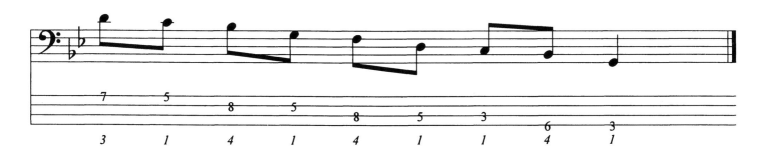

D Minor

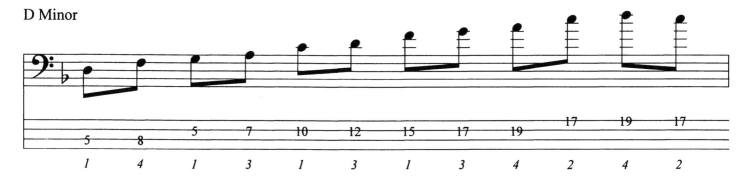

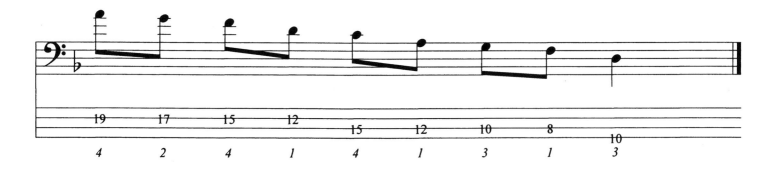